INDIAN AND ESKIMO
ART OF CANADA

INDIAN AND ESKIMO
ART OF CANADA

THE RYERSON PRESS
Toronto   Winnipeg   Vancouver

First published in 1970 by Ediciones Polígrafa, S. A. - Barcelona, (Spain)

© Ediciones Polígrafa, S. A. - Barcelona (Spain), 1970

This Canadian edition © The Ryerson Press, 1971

ISBN 0-7700-0341-9   -   PRINTED IN SPAIN

La Polígrafa, S. A. - Barcelona (Spain) - D. L. : B. 16.073 - 1970

FOTOSCOP

VISUAL LANGUAGE

Text: Ian Christie Clark

Photography: Dominique Darbois

Selection and sequence: Joan Prats Vallès

INTRODUCTION

During 1969 and 1970 an exhibition of aboriginal art from Canada was held at the Museum of Man in Paris and at the National Gallery in Ottawa. Organized by the Society of Friends of the Museum of Man in co-operation with the Canadian Government, it enabled a European audience to appreciate for the first time a representative collection of the art of the indigenous populations of Canada from the dawn of prehistory to the end of the 19th century. This exhibit, grouping masterworks from Canadian museum collections, provided a unique opportunity for the editors of the present work to create for a wider public an "Imaginary Museum" and to illustrate in book form the high level of art as practised by the first peoples who inhabited the region now known as Canada.

The first Spanish explorers who landed in the new world were able to appreciate intact the artistic traditions of the indigenous populations they encountered, but the European explorers of the 15th and 16th centuries were not artists, and even if Albrecht Dürer, the celebrated German painter, could remark[1], upon seeing the gifts from Mexico Cortez was bringing to the court of Charles Quint in 1520, that he had never seen anything quite so beautiful, a true appreciation of the art of the Americas had to await the discovery of so-called "primitive art" in the twentieth century by artists in search of a new aesthetic.

[1] As cited in "Chefs-d'oeuvre du Musée de l'Homme", Paris, 1965, page 153.

Exhibitions and collections of Pre-Colombian, African and Oceanic art have proliferated in recent years. Outside the North American continent, with few exceptions, primitive art from North America, and particularly Canada, has been less well known except as an adjunct to archaeology or ethnology and certainly less appreciated in spite of its quality. The illustrations in this volume should demonstrate to the reader, through the shock of encountering the unexpected, a source of primitive art of the highest order.

The word "primitive" applied to art risks conjuring images of ugliness and ungainliness in the public mind. But the artist of the twentieth century, in discovering artistic values in cultures other than those of Europe and the Orient, has opened our eyes and broadened our sensibilities and allowed us to appreciate qualities and dimensions foreign to our own traditions. Let the English sculptor Henry Moore[2] speak for the generation of artists, those antennae of contemporary sensibility, to whom we are indebted for our new found capacity to see beyond our traditional artistic prejudices:

> The most striking quality common to all primitive art
> is its intense vitality. It is something made by people
> with a direct and immediate response to life. Sculpture
> and painting for them were not an activity of calculation
> or academicism, but a channel for expressing powerful beliefs,
> hopes and fears.

Primitive art is a basic, elemental art, direct and forceful. It communicates, if we let it, because it speaks of elemental things. Spokesman, magician, poet for the collective unconscious of his people, the primitive artist depicted a total experience in plastic terms. We cannot penetrate the mysteries

[2] "Primitive Art", The Listener, Vol. XXV, No 641 (24 April, 1941), London, page 598.

of this experience, but if our sensibilities are not blunted, we can feel the visceral shock of creation, primaeval and universal.

It was not the intention of the editors to organize the material presented in terms of its provenance, date or culture. By turning the pages of this book the spectator will be taken on a journey through time and through space with only the object as reality and his sensibility as guide. However, a brief analysis may help the reader to orient himself.

Of the Iroquoian and Algonquin Indians of Eastern Canada, who created for the most part in perishable materials, little art remains. The first tribes to bear the brunt of European colonization and exploitation, their art rapidly suffered degenerating influences from the 18th century onwards, which explains the paucity of other than archaeological material (No 52) with which to judge the peoples immortalized by the works of James Fenimore Cooper. Note in passing the two traditionally disfigured curing masks (Nos 117 and 118) which, in spite of their deformation, express vital human emotions in plastic form.

The Indians of the Canadian prairies, Plains Cree, Blackfoot, Blood and Sioux, were able to escape an all-encompassing contamination from European influences until the beginning of the 19th century (the cinema tradition of the "Western" testifies to their agony). Buffalo hunters and warriors, adopting first the horse, of Spanish origin, from the South and later guns and trade articles from the East, they were a nomad people. Their art, as befitted a life constantly on the move following the great herds of buffalo (note the magnificent prehistoric carving from the plains, No 92), were connected with religion, war and personal adornment. The costumes (Nos 104, 110-115) show proof of an extraordinary sense of decoration, a subtle use of colour and an imaginative sense of design. This art is appealing because it diffuses something of the eternally young, the eternally childlike. But on closer examination, the buckskin costumes harmoniously decorated with beads, bells, porcupine quills, animal skins, duck bills and human hair tassels reveal the keen observation of the primitive artist who is always inspired by the natural poetry of "things".

Archaeological specimens, from the prehistoric Dorset and Thule cultures, testify to a 2,000-year-old tradition of sculpture created by the Eskimos of the Arctic regions of Canada (Nos 1, 9, 25, 40-43, 84, 93-97, 101-103, 120). Before these miniature carvings, only recently discovered by the archaeologist, we experience the same emotion as when confronted with Magdalenian art. Prehistoric art of such economy, whether of the paleolithic period in Europe or that of the proto-Eskimo, seems to suffuse a magic charge. We are in the presence of objects used to cure, to appease angry gods, to bring success in the hunt, to cast spells. With what concentration and intensity has the artist, working his walrus ivory or stone with simple bone tools over the long polar night, placed us in immediate contact with a real world of animals (Nos 93-95) as well as of men (No 120) in all its plastic solidity. What mysteries of the real world and the supernatural inextricably mixed stare back at us from the tiny sculptured masks

(Nos 1, 9, 25, 41), enigmatic and timeless. Magnified out of the miniature spirit world in which the shaman-carver has placed them, would they not reveal the plastic qualities of monumental sculpture and lose nothing of their sensitivity?

The seafaring tribes of the Northwest Coast area, the Tlingit, Haida, Tsimshian, Bella Coola, Kwakiutl and Nootka, inhabited a protected strip of indented coast between mountains and the Pacific Ocean. These master wood carvers were discovered by European explorers only at the end of the 18th century. They had long developed a social structure which they felt compelled to express in visual and plastic terms resulting in primitive art which is perhaps among the most refined known. The impulse to visualize the sacred and supernatural world in wood and paint (the magic realm of the ceremonial spirit masks) combined with an urge to visualize profane worldly rivalries, art testifying to pride of rank (crests and costumes), of lineage (totemic carving and monumental sculpture), as well as of wealth and prestige (finely worked articles of everyday life). The result was a culture obsessed with art in which the woodworking craftsman, really a "professional" artist, played a predominant and privileged role. European contact, restricted for a long period during the 19th century to trade rather than colonization or even evangelism, stimulated artistic creation without corrupting native styles. New wealth created new demands and new tools facilitated technical virtuosity which created a climate of artistic ferment comparable to the Renaissance in Europe. What remains of this artistic heritage (wood decays rapidly in a humid climate) has moved the French anthropologist Lévi-

Strauss to compare it to the art of ancient Egypt and archaic Greece[3].

Two traditional modes of artistic expression can be discerned in Northwest Coast art: the three-dimensional search for plastic form, the essence of sculpture; and the two-dimensional search for pictorial representation, the essence of painting. Compare the plastic simplicity of the Tsimshian stone mask (No 57) with the riot of symbolic decoration, double-imaged and filling the design field, of the painted house partition (Nos 64 and 65) and the woven Tlingit dance tunic (No 31). The two traditions interweave and blend under varying degrees of tension. Compare the Haida and Tsimshian shaman rattles: in the first (No 54),

[3] As quoted in the "Bulletin", Canadian Commission for Unesco, Vol. 12, No 3 (October, 1969), Ottawa, page 4.

surface decoration is pushing into form; in the second (No 90), form is heightened by decoration. In examining the monumental totemic sculpture (general view, Nos 2 and 3 and detail, Nos 28 and 29), we observe the influence of the painter's technique not as decoration, but as two-dimensional flat design curved around the tree-trunk and carved in three-dimensional relief. In the most subtle examples of this art, all the available space is worked and the view of the beholder, as if on the flux of some invisible tide, is drawn from the flat surface into volume and then pulled back again to linear design.

To know a man we search his face to penetrate the mask he offers to the world. The artist of the Northwest Coast literally peopled his art with faces. We encounter classical human faces (No 58), animal faces (No 10), demon faces (No 18), anthropo-morphic faces (No 19). Some seem possessed (Nos 14, 59) and some "transform" theatrically before our eyes (Nos 20-24). During the Winter festivals the masks did not merely represent demons or spirits. Through a process of "transubstantiation" the wood became flesh for the faithful. We sense this troubling power in searching these mask-faces which peer and glare out at us, wrenched from their esoteric rituals. We cannot know them, but if our senses are in a state of grace, they too can speak to us, through the magic of art, of the universality of mankind.

2

3

5

14

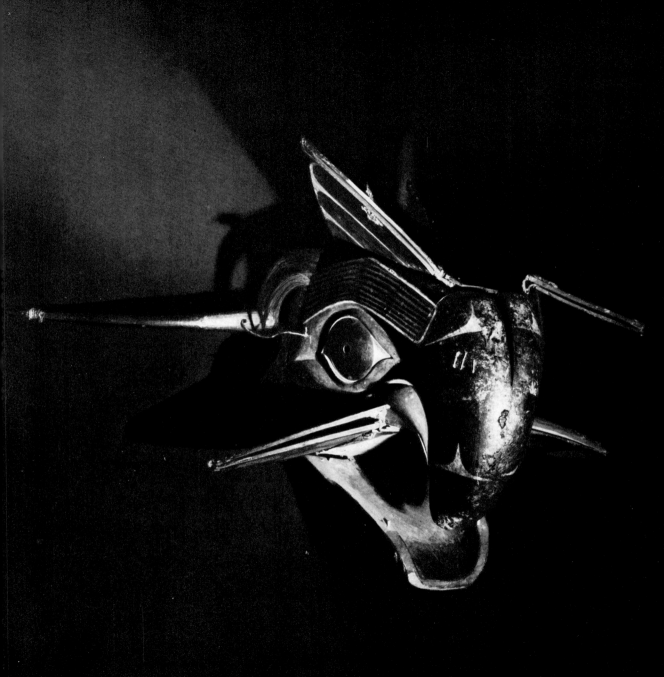

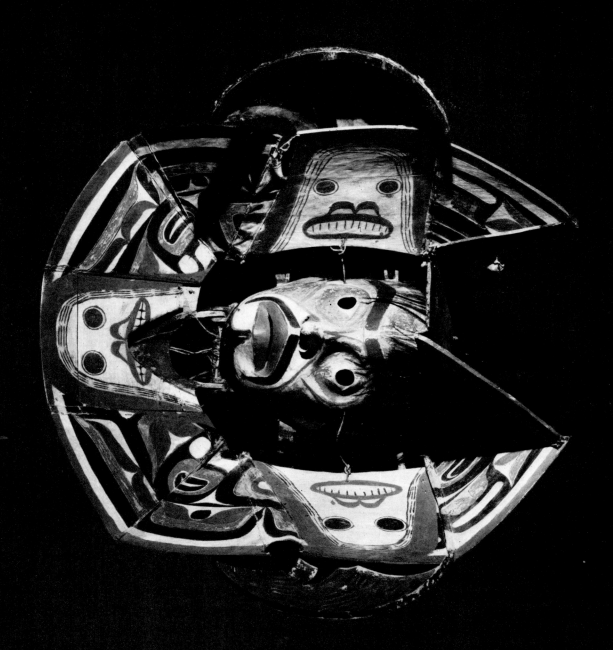

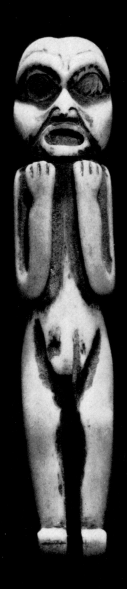

58

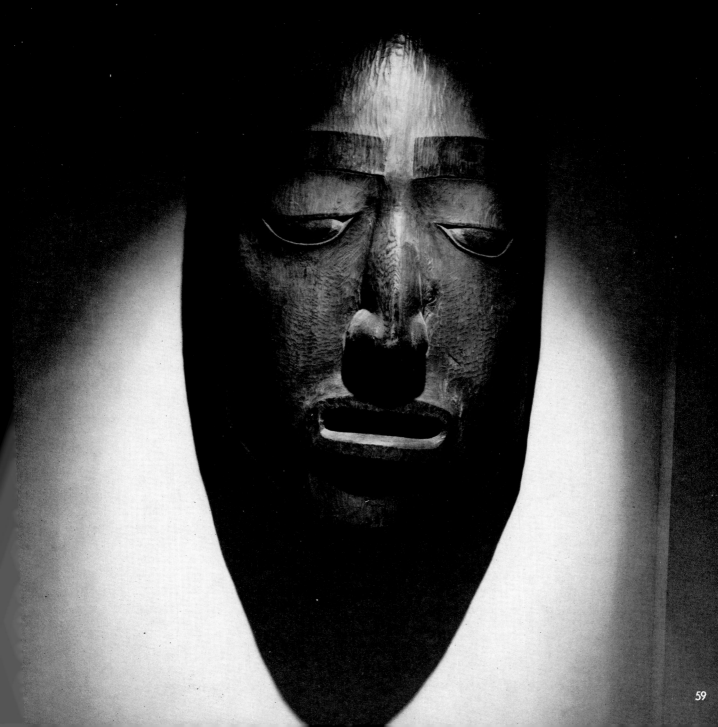

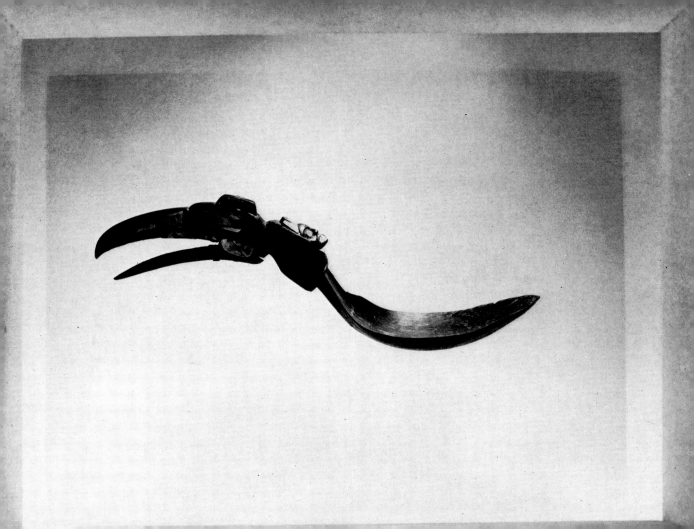

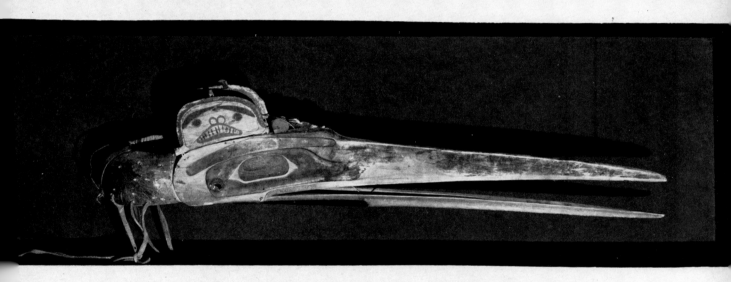

87

89

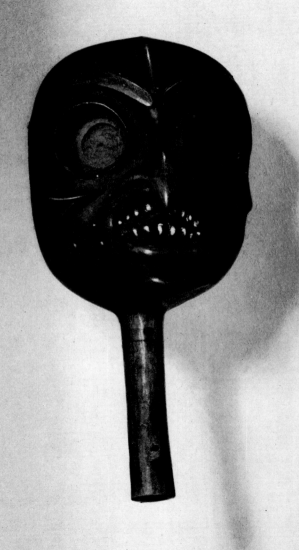

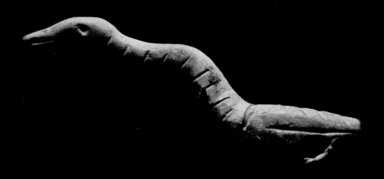

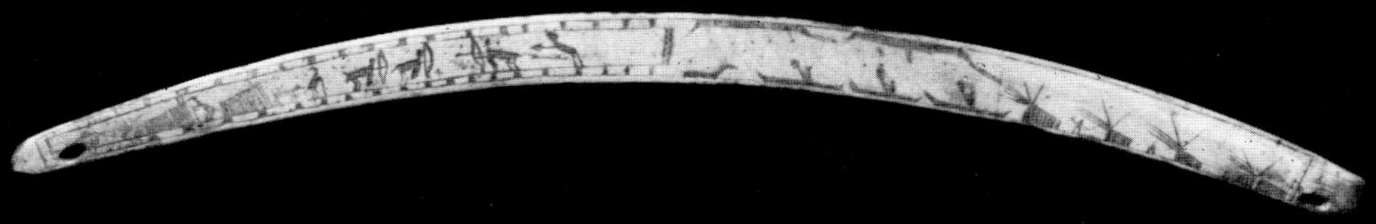

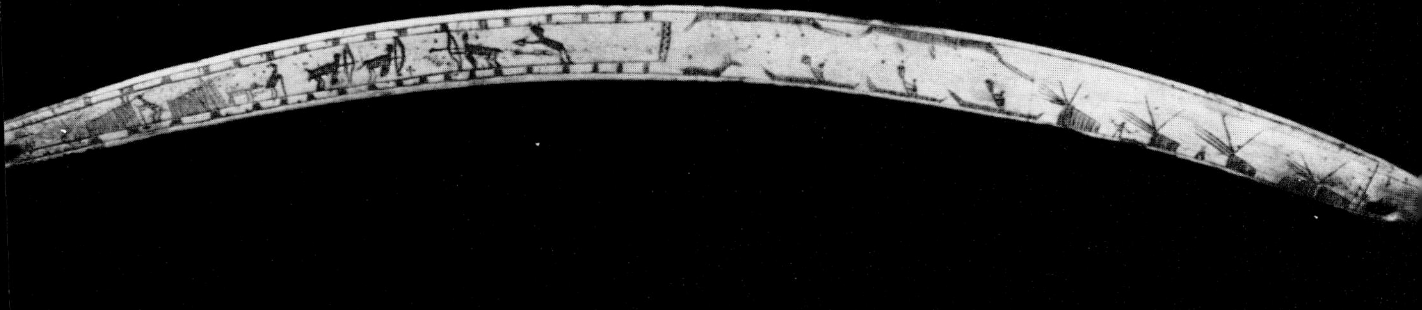

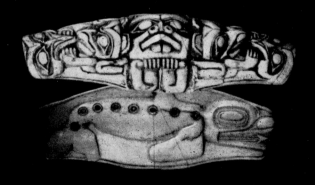

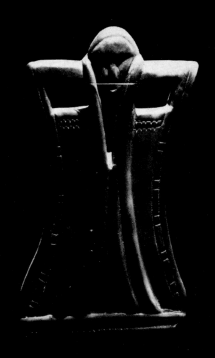

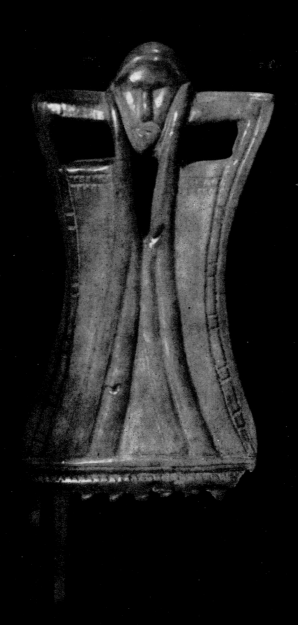

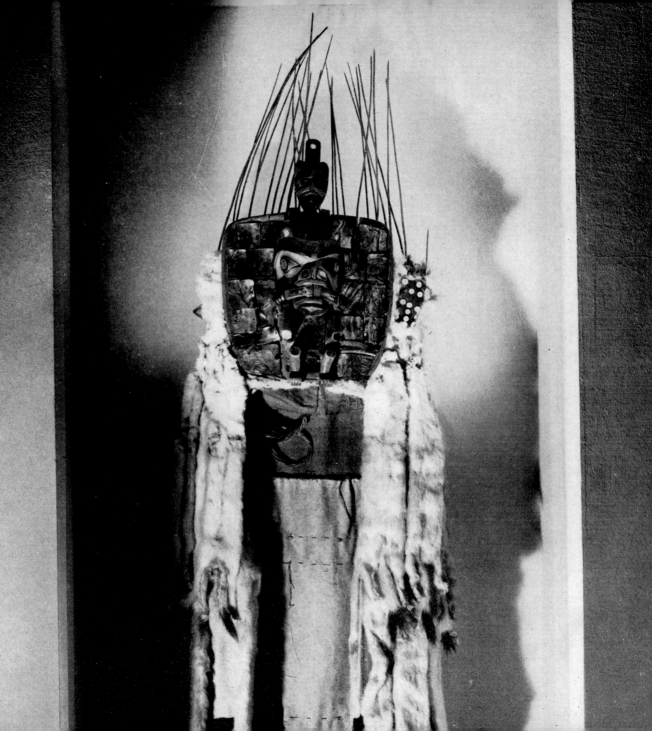